THE GREAT CHICAGO FIRE

Robin Johnson

CRABTREE
Publishing Company
www.crabtreebooks.com

Crabtree Publishing Company
www.crabtreebooks.com

Author: Robin Johnson
**Publishing plan research
    and development**: Reagan Miller
Project coordinator: Crystal Sikkens
Editors: Sonya Newland, Crystal Sikkens
Proofreader: Janine Deschenes
Original design: Tim Mayer (Mayer Media)
Book design: Clare Nicholas
Cover design: Ken Wright
Map: Stefan Chabluk
**Production coordinator and
    prepress technician**: Ken Wright
Print coordinator: Margaret Amy Salter
Production coordinated by:
    White-Thomson Publishing

Photographs:
Alamy: Glasshouse Images: pp. 16–17, 32; North
Wind Picture Archive: pp. 19, 20, 22–23, 30–31;
Interfoto: pp. 21, 34; Bridgeman Art Library: The
Great Chicago Fire of 1871, Dear, Neville
(b.1923)/Private Collection/© Look and Learn:
pp. 24–25; Corbis: Bettmann: p. 36; Getty Images:
Chicago History Museum: pp. 4–5, 14–15, 37;
Library of Congress: cover, pp. 1, 18, 26–27, 29, 35;
Shutterstock: Everett Historical: pp. 3, 9, 12–13,
13, 28–29, 38-39; Papa Bravo: p. 42; EQRoy: p. 43;
Pigprox: p. 45; Topfoto: The Granger Collection:
pp. 10–11; Wikimedia: pp. 6–7, 8, 33, 40; J.
Crocker: p. 41; Thshriver: p. 44.

Library and Archives Canada Cataloguing in Publication

Johnson, Robin (Robin R.), author
        The great Chicago fire / Robin Johnson.

(Crabtree chrome)
Includes index.
Issued in print and electronic formats.
ISBN 978-0-7787-2296-0 (bound).--ISBN 978-0-7787-2235-9
(paperback).--ISBN 978-1-4271-8090-2 (html)

        1. Great Fire, Chicago, Ill., 1871--Juvenile literature.
2. Fires--Illinois--Chicago--History--19th century--Juvenile
literature. 3. Chicago (Ill.)--History--To 1875--Juvenile literature.
I. Title. II. Series: Crabtree chrome

F548.42.J65 2016   j977.3'11041   C2015-907962-4
                                            C2015-907963-2

Library of Congress Cataloging-in-Publication Data

CIP available at Library of Congress

Crabtree Publishing Company

www.crabtreebooks.com   1-800-387-7650

Printed in Canada/022016/MA20151130

Published in Canada
Crabtree Publishing
616 Welland Ave.
St. Catharines, ON
L2M 5V6

Published in the United States
Crabtree Publishing
PMB 59051
350 Fifth Avenue, 59th Floor
New York, New York 10118

Published in the United Kingdom
Crabtree Publishing
Maritime House
Basin Road North, Hove
BN41 1WR

Published in Australia
Crabtree Publishing
3 Charles Street
Coburg North
VIC 3058

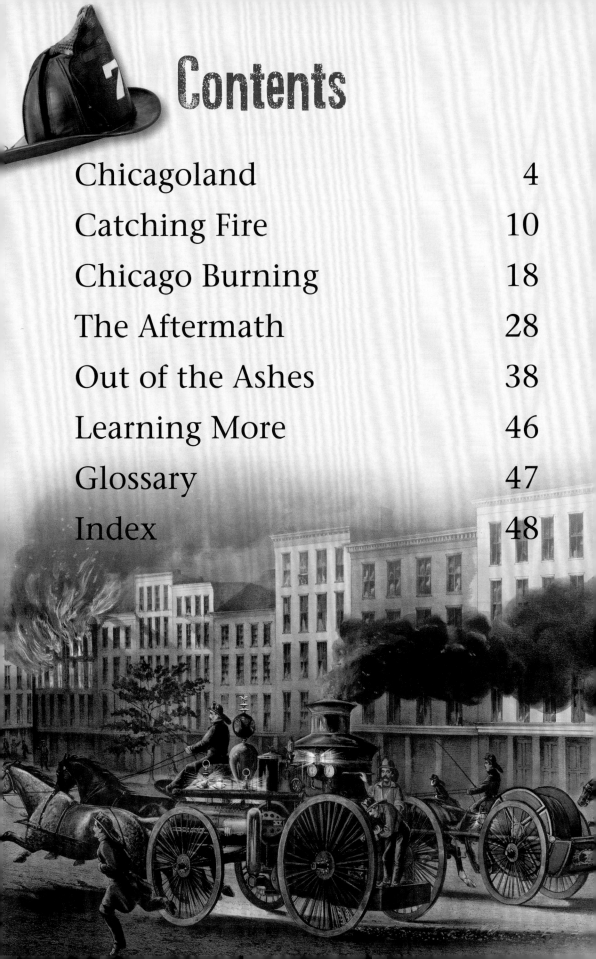

Contents

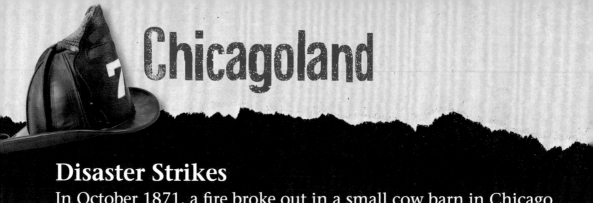

Chicagoland

Disaster Strikes

In October 1871, a fire broke out in a small cow barn in Chicago. The flames grew and spread quickly to nearby buildings. Firefighters rushed to the scene and battled the blaze, but they could not stop it. Soon, the deadly fire was raging through the city.

▼ *Thousands of people were forced from their homes as fire swept through the streets of Chicago.*

Chicago Burning

Families grabbed their belongings and ran for their lives. They screamed and pushed their way through the crowded city streets. The fire spread faster and faster. The flames leapt higher and higher. Chicago was burning! Fire! Fire! Fire!

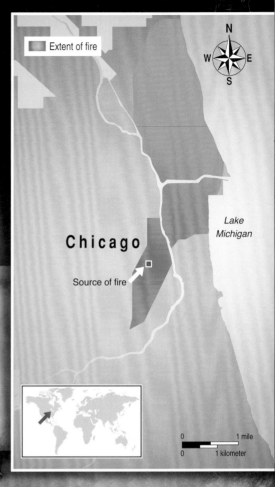

Extent of fire

N
W — E
S

Lake Michigan

Chicago

Source of fire

0 ___ 1 mile
0 ___ 1 kilometer

▶ *This is a map of Chicago in 1871. The colored part shows the area damaged by the Great Fire. The dot shows where the fire is believed to have started.*

The Great Chicago Fire was one of the worst **disasters** of the century. It destroyed buildings, bridges, and roads. Hundreds of people lost their lives. Many more lost everything they owned.

disasters: sudden accidents that cause great loss

The Early Settlers

The first settler came to Chicago in the 1780s. A trader named Jean Baptiste Point du Sable made his home at the mouth of the Chicago River. By 1833, about 200 people lived in Chicago. Within a few years, it had become a busy city of 4,000 people. After that, Chicago just kept growing.

▼ *This picture shows Chicago in 1833, when it was little more than a village by the river.*

Chicago is called the Windy City. Strong winds blow from Lake Michigan and whip through the city streets. The wind would cause a fire to spread quickly.

The Center of It All

By the 1850s, Chicago was **booming**. Located in Illinois, near the middle of the United States, the city was a busy trade and transportation center. Trains and ships from around the country met in Chicago. They brought factory goods from the East and crops from the West.

booming: doing well and growing fast

Lumber Capital

In the late 1800s, Chicago was the lumber capital of the world. The city was located near the thick forests of the Upper Great Lakes. **Chicagoans** cut down trees and shipped the wood across the country. They also used lumber to grow their own city. Using wood allowed Chicagoans to build quickly and cheaply. But wood catches fire and burns easily.

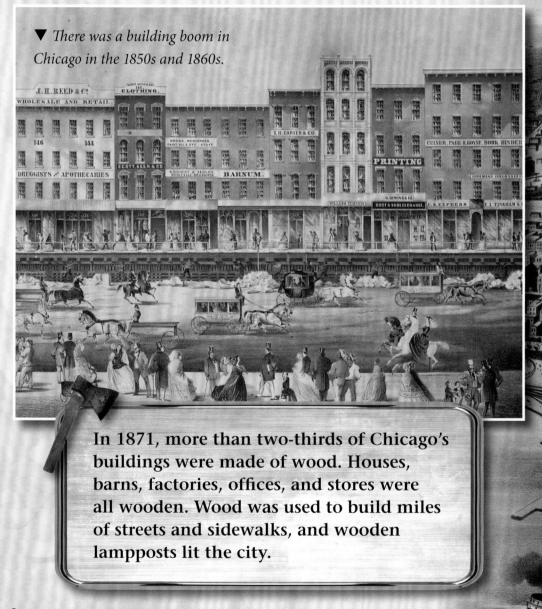

▼ *There was a building boom in Chicago in the 1850s and 1860s.*

In 1871, more than two-thirds of Chicago's buildings were made of wood. Houses, barns, factories, offices, and stores were all wooden. Wood was used to build miles of streets and sidewalks, and wooden lampposts lit the city.

Boom Town

By 1871, about 300,000 people lived in Chicago. It was one of the largest cities in the United States. There were more than 1,100 factories there. Department stores sold goods of all kinds. Chicago's booming businesses created high hopes for the future. It seemed that nothing could slow the progress of this growing city.

▼ *Before the fire, Chicago was a big, busy city.*

Chicagoans: people who live in Chicago

Catching Fire

Mrs. O'Leary's Cow

On Sunday, October 8, around 9:00 p.m., a fire broke out at 137 DeKoven Street in the west end of Chicago. The story goes that a woman named Catherine O'Leary was milking her cows before bed. She was using an oil lamp to light her small barn. A cow kicked over the lantern and some straw caught fire. Soon the entire barn was up in flames.

Barnyard Blaze

A neighbor named Daniel "Peg Leg" Sullivan spotted the fire first. He rushed to free the animals trapped in the barn. He could save only a calf from the flames. Then Peg Leg began shouting—*Fire! Fire! Fire!* The flames spread quickly from the barn. There were small wooden houses and sheds packed tightly all around. Before long, they were all on fire.

◀ *Few people had electricity in the nineteenth century. Most used lamps with fire in them as lights.*

The famous cow tale may not be true. The fire began in the barn, but Mrs. O'Leary claimed she was in bed at the time. The people of Chicago wanted someone to blame for the disaster. Mrs. O'Leary—a poor Irish **immigrant**—was an easy choice.

immigrant: someone who goes to live in a new country

First Responders

A watchman in the courthouse tower spotted the fire. He sent firefighters right away—but to the wrong place! The fire crew showed up at another spot instead. By the time the steam engines arrived at the O'Leary barn, the small fire had become a **conflagration**.

▼ *Fire engines were usually pulled by horses. There were often separate carts for the ladders and hoses.*

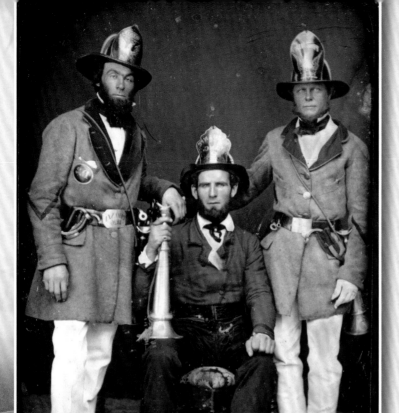

◄ *In the nineteenth century, firefighters did not have the equipment or protective clothing that they use today.*

Too Little Too Late

The firefighters tried hard to contain the growing fire. They were exhausted from fighting a number of fires that week, however. The city had only 185 firefighters and 17 horse-drawn fire engines. It was not nearly enough to stop the mighty fire from spreading.

"It was a grand sight, and yet an awful one."

William Gallagher, a student in Chicago

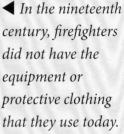

conflagration: a huge fire that causes a lot of damage

13

Growing Fire

Strong winds carried the flames quickly to the east and north. The fire leapt from house to house and street to street. In less than ten minutes, it had covered two city blocks. Then the fire headed straight for Chicago's main business district.

Growing Fear

At first, curious onlookers stood and watched buildings burn. Fires were common in the wooden city and no one was too worried about this one. Then people began to realize that this fire was different. It was quickly moving toward them—and firefighters could not stop it.

◄ *People watched with interest as firefighters tried to tackle the blaze.*

The weather in Chicago that year made it **vulnerable** to fire. There had been almost no rain for several months. This left the wooden buildings dry and easy to burn. The wind was strong in the Windy City that night. It helped the fire spread quickly.

vulnerable: open to attack or harm

▼ *Some people put on their best clothes so they would not have to carry them.*

Packing It In

People rushed to pack their belongings. They had just minutes to save them from the flames. Some people took jewelry, silver, family photos, Bibles, and other prized possessions. Some packed food, blankets, and other useful items. Others began to panic and grabbed whatever they could carry. One woman saved her wedding **veil**. Another took a pot of soup!

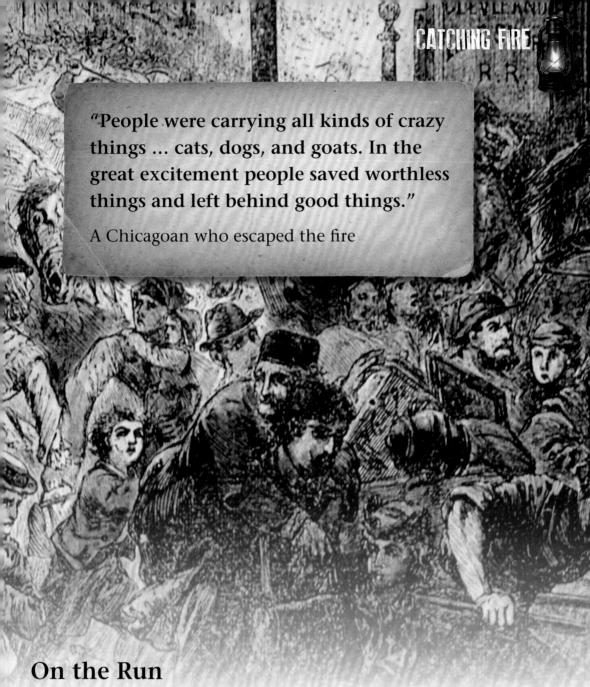

"People were carrying all kinds of crazy things ... cats, dogs, and goats. In the great excitement people saved worthless things and left behind good things."

A Chicagoan who escaped the fire

On the Run

Some wealthy families loaded their belongings onto horse-drawn wagons and paid drivers to take them to safety. The wagons did not get far in the crowded city streets. Some drivers stole what they could carry and left the rest to burn. Many families struck out on foot with their children, pets, and belongings in their arms. Some even carried bed mattresses on their heads! They ran from their homes and prayed for the best.

veil: a light, see-through covering that a bride wears over her face

Up in Flames

The fire raged wildly out of control. Strong winds caused rising flames to twist and twirl. The fast-spinning flames—called fire whirls—ripped the roofs off buildings. They also spit burning **debris** in all directions, which set more buildings on fire. Flames raced toward the busy city center. The Chicago River stood in their way, however. The fire could not cross the water. Or could it?

▶ *The building that housed the city's newspaper, the* Chicago Tribune, *was destroyed by the fire.*

"The fire was moving northward like ocean surf on a sand beach. ... A column of flame would shoot up from a burning building, catch the force of the wind, and strike the next one."

Horace White, editor of the *Chicago Tribune* newspaper

Over the River

The fire roared over the city's wooden bridges. It spread to boats that were docked closely together on the water. Waste and oil floating on the surface of the river caught fire. Fire whirls sent heat and flaming chunks of wood across the water. By 11:30 p.m., the fire had crossed the river into the heart of Chicago.

▼ *Even the river could not stop the fire from spreading right into the center of the city.*

debris: pieces of wrecked objects

Going Downtown

The fire ripped through the downtown streets of Chicago. Wooden building after building went up in flames. The fire took department stores, offices, factories, hotels, theaters, banks, and churches. Even the wooden sidewalks and roads caught fire! Smoke rose up and red-hot ashes rained down on the people who tried to **flee** the city.

▼ Ashes burned and choked people as they tried to escape.

"It was like a snowstorm only the flakes were red instead of white."

Thirteen-year-old Bessie Bradwell Helmer, describing the falling ashes

▲ *Some people
jumped out of windows as
the fire took hold of their houses.*

Fleeing the Flames

People screamed as they tried to outrun the fast-moving fire. Some fell down in their hurry to escape the heat and flames. They were trampled by the crowd or crushed by falling debris. Some dropped their belongings, or were separated from their families. But there was no turning back.

flee: to run away from a place of danger

Explosion!

Around midnight, the city's gasworks exploded. The gasworks was a factory where coal was made into gas for heating and cooking. The huge explosion rocked the city and fueled the fire with **flammable** gas. It also left most of the city in the dark. Flaming lampposts and buildings helped light the way.

▼ *The courthouse bell had been sounding the alarm as the flames spread, but that stopped when the building caught fire.*

The City Falls

Soon, other important buildings came crashing down. The courthouse caught fire around 1:30 a.m. Then the waterworks went up in flames. It was the building that stored Chicago's water supply. The city's main source of drinking water was no longer usable—and the pumps used to fight fires were destroyed.

When the courthouse caught fire, the prisoners locked inside were set free. They may have gotten a lucky break—or died in the fire that raged outside the jail.

flammable: easily set on fire

Burning Bridges

As the city burned to the ground, Chicagoans kept fleeing. They had to get out of there—or get burned alive. They rushed to bridges around the city. The bridges were clogged with people, horses, and wagons. Everyone pushed and shoved and fought their way across the river. One by one, the bridges were blocked by the fire, however.

"The rail of the bridge was broken away. How many people were pushed over the bridge into the water I cannot tell. I myself saw one man stumble under a load of clothing and disappear."

Alexander Frear

▼ *As more and more of the city caught fire, Chicagoans did not know where to turn to escape.*

Nowhere to Run

By the early morning of Monday, October 9, Chicagoans had nowhere left to run. The fire had forced thousands of people east—straight to the shores of Lake Michigan. Families **huddled** together with their belongings piled around them. Some waded into the icy water to escape the heat. Others drove their horses and wagons right into the lake!

huddled: crowded together in a group

Still Fighting

Later that morning, General Philip H. Sheridan took action. He ordered his troops to blow up the buildings on Michigan Avenue. The fire would slow down if it had nothing to burn or fuel the flames. Families stood and watched as their fine homes were flattened. Other buildings around the city were also blown up. But the fire had spread so far and wide that even an army and gunpowder could not stop it.

"There was no sleep for us until we heard the welcome sound of rain against our windows. How our hearts did rise in thankfulness to heaven for rain!"

Horace White, who took shelter in his brother's cottage after his own house burned down

Rain at Last

The Great Chicago Fire raged on for nearly 30 hours. On Monday night, the city got lucky and finally got some rain. Families cried tears of joy as rain began to fall and put out the flames. By the morning of Tuesday, October 10, the rain had **extinguished** the fire at last. The conflagration was finally over. But the damage had been done.

▼ *After more than a day, rain finally helped put out the fire— but the city was in ruins.*

extinguished: put out a fire

The Aftermath

The Smoke Clears

When the smoke cleared, Chicagoans surveyed the damage. They were shocked by what they saw. Their mighty city was in ruins! The downtown had gone down in flames. Its tall buildings lay in heaps of steaming rubble. The broken city continued to **smolder** for several days.

> "The busy, peopled streets, the pleasant stores with their wide inviting doors, with cheerful [welcoming] gentlemen within…are now stumbling pathways, through heaps of blackened bricks and dusty ashes, with silent people wandering among the ruins."
>
> James W. Milner, describing the ruins

▼ *Small fires continued to burn in parts of Chicago for days after the conflagration ended.*

The Burnt District

The massive fire had taken one-third of the city. More than 17,000 buildings had been destroyed in an area now called the Burnt District. Miles of roads and sidewalks had gone up in flames. In all, the fire destroyed about 200 million dollars of property. That would be more than four billion dollars of damage today.

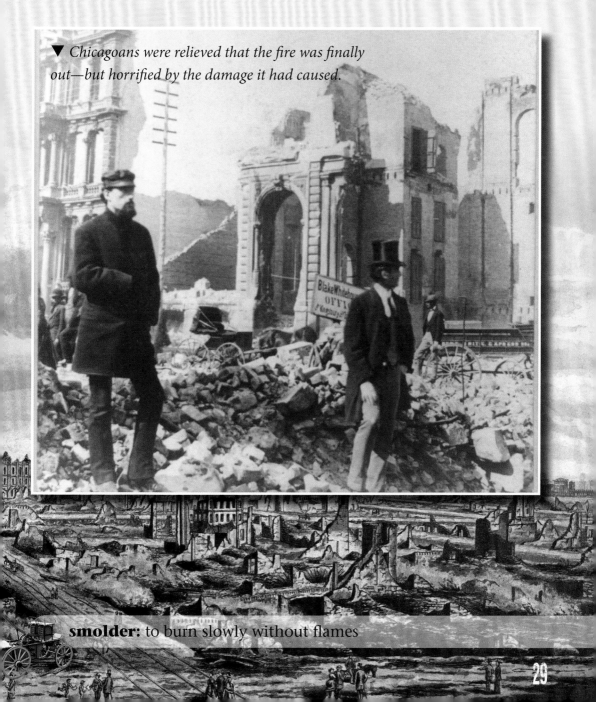

▼ *Chicagoans were relieved that the fire was finally out—but horrified by the damage it had caused.*

smolder: to burn slowly without flames

The Dead

As many as 300 people died in the Great Chicago Fire. Many of the victims were found in Conley's Patch. It was a poor part of the city where Irish immigrants lived. The fire hit this crowded area with little warning and spread quickly through the small, flimsy shacks.

The Great Chicago Fire was not the only deadly blaze on October 8, 1871. Several major fires began around Lake Michigan that same day. The deadliest was a forest fire in Peshtigo, Wisconsin. It killed more than 1,500 people and remains the worst fire in American history.

The Missing

Some of the fire's victims were never seen again.
Families searched the city for missing loved ones,
but with little hope. They may have drowned in the
river and been washed away, or the red-hot flames
may have completely **incinerated** their bodies.

▼ *People walked among the ruins, unable to
believe how much damage had been done.*

incinerated: burned to ashes

Homeless in Chicago

Many Chicagoans found themselves suddenly homeless. About 100,000 people—a third of the city's **population**—had lost their houses in the blaze. The finest mansions and the poorest shacks had all burned to the ground. The homeless gathered together in scared, stunned groups outside the city. Where would they live? What would they do now?

▼ *After the fire, people were forced to live in makeshift shelters on the outskirts of the city.*

"The Homestead built by my own hands out of my own hard earnings, is gone—a total wreck."

Letter from fire survivor William Carter

Give Me Shelter

The homeless would have to rebuild their lives in Chicago. But first, they had to stay alive. Winter was coming and soon the weather would turn cold in the Windy City. They needed shelter right away. Some families pitched tents or built shacks among the rubble. Others moved into churches and public buildings outside the Burnt District.

▶ *This poster tells people that they can find shelter in schools and other public buildings if they lost their homes in the fire.*

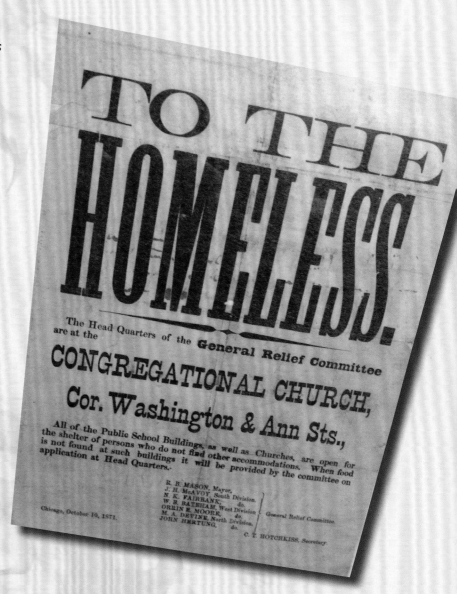

population: the number of people living in an area

The Kindness of Strangers

News of the disaster spread quickly. Soon, help was pouring in from other parts of the United States and around the world. People **donated** money, food, water, fuel, candles, clothing, books, and other items. They sent thousands of sewing machines so people could make clothes for their families. They also donated firefighting equipment to help Chicago prevent another disaster.

▼ *People rushed to help the poor Chicagoans. These women are handing out donated food to poor children.*

Law and Order

Not everyone was willing to wait for handouts, however. Some Chicagoans broke into buildings outside the Burnt District and stole the supplies they needed. The mayor of Chicago, Roswell B. Mason, ordered martial law to keep the peace. That meant the city was controlled by armed forces instead of the police. The city remained under the army's command for several days.

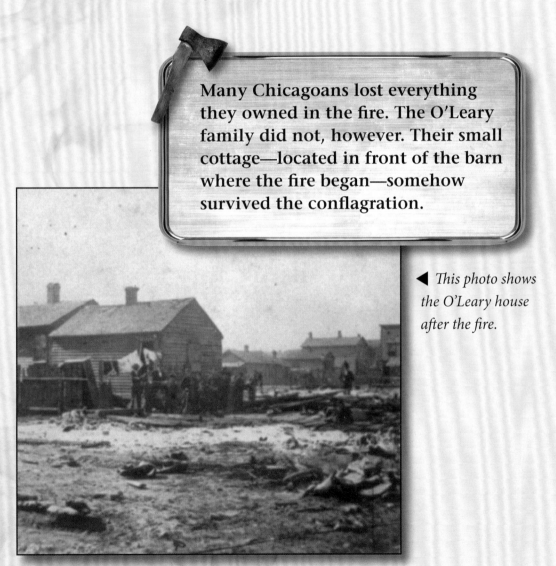

Many Chicagoans lost everything they owned in the fire. The O'Leary family did not, however. Their small cottage—located in front of the barn where the fire began—somehow survived the conflagration.

◀ *This photo shows the O'Leary house after the fire.*

donated: gave money or goods to people in need

Repair and Rebuild

Chicagoans were eager to repair and rebuild their city. Men cleared the heavy rubble from the roads. Most of the docks and railroad tracks were intact, so donated goods and building supplies could be sent to the city by ship or train. The first load of lumber arrived the day the fire was put out. Soon, wooden shacks and stands had sprung up among the ruins.

▼ *William D. Kerfoot was the first Chicagoan to get back to business. The day after the fire ended, the real estate dealer built a small wooden office among the rubble.*

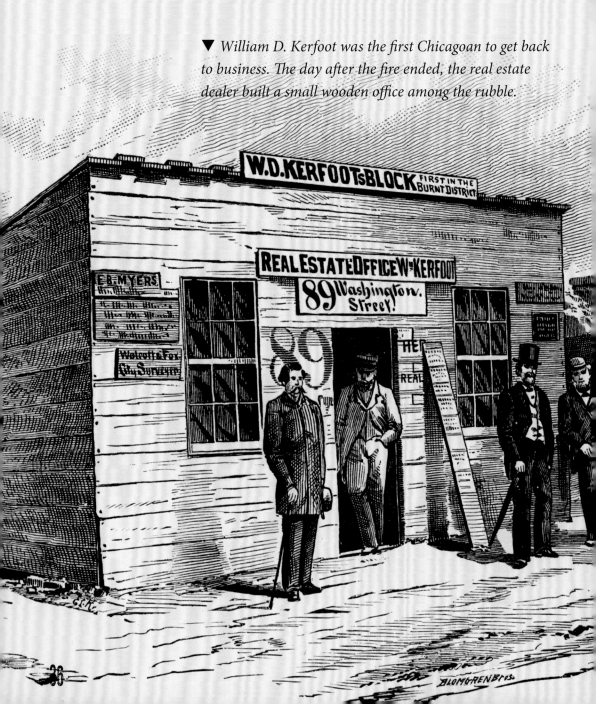

Business as Usual

Thousands of Chicagoans returned to their jobs in mills and lumberyards. Most of Chicago's industries were located outside the city center, so they survived the fire. Industries turn raw materials, such as grain or wood, into goods for sale. Chicago's industries and farms helped keep its **economy** growing after the disaster.

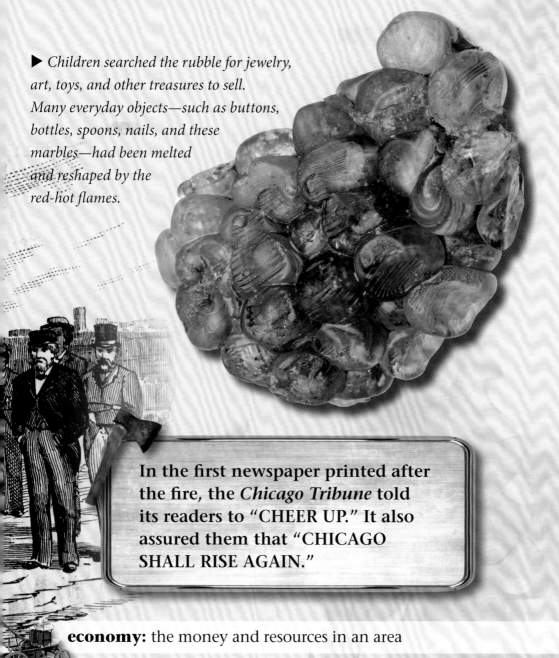

▶ *Children searched the rubble for jewelry, art, toys, and other treasures to sell. Many everyday objects—such as buttons, bottles, spoons, nails, and these marbles—had been melted and reshaped by the red-hot flames.*

In the first newspaper printed after the fire, the *Chicago Tribune* told its readers to "CHEER UP." It also assured them that "CHICAGO SHALL RISE AGAIN."

economy: the money and resources in an area

Out of the Ashes

New Laws

After the fire, new building laws were passed in Chicago. The laws forced builders to use brick, stone, steel, and other **fireproof** materials. These materials were much more expensive than wood. Not everyone in Chicago could afford to buy them. Some poor families had no choice but to leave the city. Other people ignored the new laws and built wooden homes and businesses.

▼ *Within two years, Chicago had risen from the ashes and was a booming city once again.*

Disaster Strikes Twice

Chicagoans kept rebuilding their city—until two sad events stopped their progress. In 1873, a depression hit North America. A depression is a period of time when businesses fail and many workers do not have jobs. Many Chicagoans could not afford to build new homes—or even keep the ones they had. On July 14, 1874, another fire swept through Chicago. It destroyed more than 800 buildings and killed 20 people.

Chicagoans were eager to rebuild their city after the Great Fire. Luckily, they had a solid foundation to build it on. Many of the city's basic structures and services had survived the blaze.

fireproof: unable to catch fire

Fireproof City

After the fire in 1874, Chicagoans began to realize the importance of using fireproof materials to rebuild their city. They started using materials such as steel and terra-cotta. Terra-cotta is a strong, brown-orange clay used to make building tiles. It helped make Chicago one of the most fireproof cities in America by the mid-1880s.

▲ *The Palmer House claimed to be "The World's Only Fireproof Hotel." The grand hotel was rebuilt in 1875 using brick, iron, and terra-cotta.*

The Chicago School

The **architecture** of Chicago also changed after the Great Fire. Business owners wanted tall buildings with natural light and simple, streamlined styles. Building materials were expensive and they did not want to pay extra money for fancy decorations. The group of architects who developed this new building design was known as the Chicago School. Their name was soon used to refer to this design.

▶ *The Chicago Building was designed by the Chicago School and built in 1904. It has a metal frame and the outside is covered in terra-cotta.*

The Chicago School designed the world's first skyscraper, which was built in 1885. A skyscraper is a very tall building in a city. The Home Insurance Building was 10 stories tall and had a fireproof steel frame.

architecture: the art of designing and creating buildings

Chicago Today

Today, Chicago is the third-largest city in the United States. More than 2.7 million people live there. The city is known for its architecture and tall buildings. Skyscrapers tower above the busy streets. Chicago's Willis Tower is the second-tallest building in the country.

In 1956, a training school for firefighters was built on DeKoven Street in Chicago. This school, called the Robert J. Quinn Fire Academy, is located where the O'Leary barn once stood— and where the Great Chicago Fire began.

▼ *Chicago's Cloud Gate sculpture reflects how far the city has come since the Great Fire.*

Fire and Water

The Chicago Water Tower stands proud among the city's skyscrapers. It is one of the few buildings that survived the disaster of 1871. The tower was used to fight fires at the time. Today, it is a symbol of the city's **tragic** past, its fiery spirit, and its hopes for the future.

▲ *The Chicago Water Tower was built in 1869, two years before the Great Fire.*

tragic: very sad

43

Remembering the Fire

The people of Chicago have put the tragic event far behind them. But they will never forget it. Over the years, Chicagoans have **commemorated** the fire with parades, concerts, fireworks, and festivals. In 1961, a bronze statue of flames, known as the Pillar of Fire, was built in front of the Robert J. Quinn Fire Academy, on the spot where the Great Chicago Fire began.

◀ *The Pillar of Fire is a lasting reminder of the conflagration and its victims.*

Fire Prevention Week commemorates the Great Chicago Fire. Each year around October 9, people in the United States and Canada learn about fire safety and how to prevent future disasters.

Burning Questions

In 1997, the city of Chicago found Mrs. O'Leary—and her cow—not guilty of starting the fire. So how did it begin? Could it have been a spark from Peg Leg Sullivan's pipe? Or maybe children knocked over a lantern while playing cards in the barn. Some believe a fiery comet may have fallen to Earth and sparked several deadly fires that night. We may never know how the Great Chicago Fire really started. But we do know that it ended in disaster.

▲ *The city has been rebuilt from the rubble, but the people of Chicago will always remember the disaster.*

commemorated: did something special to honor the past

Books

Fire: Chicago, 1871 (Survivors)
by Kathleen Duey and
Karen A. Bale
(Aladdin, 2014)

*I Survived: The Great
Chicago Fire, 1871*
by Lauren Tarshis
(Scholastic Inc., 2015)

*Surviving the Great
Chicago Fire* (Eye on History
Graphic Illustrated)
by Jo Cleland
(Rourke Publishing, 2011)

The Great Chicago Fire
(Code Red)
by Janet McHugh
(Bearport Publishing, 2007)

The Great Fire
by Jim Murphy
(Scholastic Paperbacks, 2010)

*The Great Peshtigo Fire: Stories
and Science from America's
Deadliest Fire*
by Scott Knickelbine
(Wisconsin Historical
Society Press, 2012)

Websites

www.greatchicagofire.org/
Chicago History Museum: The
Great Chicago Fire & the Web
of Memory

**www.pbs.org/wgbh/amex/
chicago/maps/**
PBS American Experience:
Chicago on Fire!

**http://education.
nationalgeographic.com/
news/chicago-fire-1871-and-
great-rebuilding/**
National Geographic: The
Chicago Fire of 1871 and the
"Great Rebuilding"

**www.nfpa.org/safety-
information/fire-prevention-
week/about-fire-prevention-
week**
Fire Prevention Safety Week
site by National Fire Protection
Association

Glossary

architecture The art of designing and creating buildings

booming Doing well and growing fast

Chicagoans People who live in Chicago

commemorated Did something special to honor the past

conflagration A huge fire that causes a lot of damage

debris Pieces of wrecked objects

disasters Sudden accidents that cause great loss

donated Gave money or goods to people in need

economy The money and resources in an area

extinguished Put out a fire

fireproof Unable to catch fire

flammable Easily set on fire

flee To run away from a place of danger

huddled Crowded together in a group

immigrant Someone who goes to live in a new country

incinerated Burned to ashes

population The number of people living in an area

smolder To burn slowly without flames

tragic Very sad

veil A light, see-through covering that a bride wears over her face

vulnerable Open to attack or harm

Index

Entries in **bold** refer to pictures